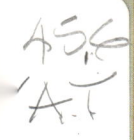
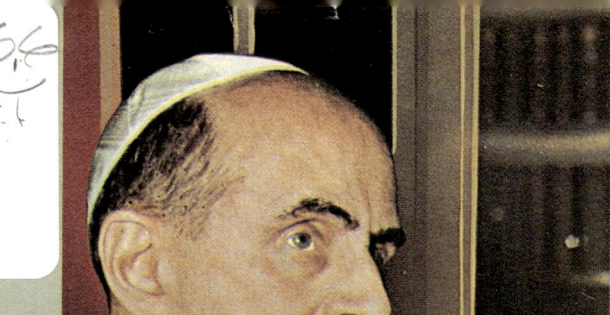
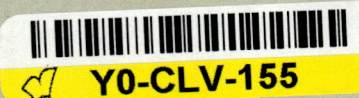

DEDICATION

It was beloved Pope John XXIII who, upon being informed of the invitation to the Vatican to participate in the New York World's Fair and learning of its theme "Peace through Understanding," enthusiastically proposed to the Bishops of the United States the construction of the Vatican Pavilion.

To the happy memory, then, of that lovable Pope of Peace and Unity and, in devotion to and esteem for His Holiness, Paul VI, his gloriously reigning successor to the Chair of St. Peter, this volume of the sights and scenes of Vatican City is dedicated.

THE PIETA FOLIO

From the day just before the turn of the 15th Century when youthful Michelangelo completed the Pieta, the permanent home of this lovely sculpture has been the Basilica of St. Peter in Rome.

Two years ago, Pope John XXIII acquiesed to the request of His Eminence, Francis Cardinal Spellman, that the Pieta be permitted to journey to the United States so that millions of Americans who might otherwise never see it could view this priceless treasure. Pope Paul VI confirmed the action of his predecessor. Thus, this superb homage in marble to Christianity came to grace the Vatican Pavilion at the New York World's Fair.

This eight-page folio humbly presents in full stature and in various details, the Crown Jewel of the Vatican Pavilion—the Pieta, Sorrowful Mother at the foot of the Cross, by Michelangelo Buonarroti.

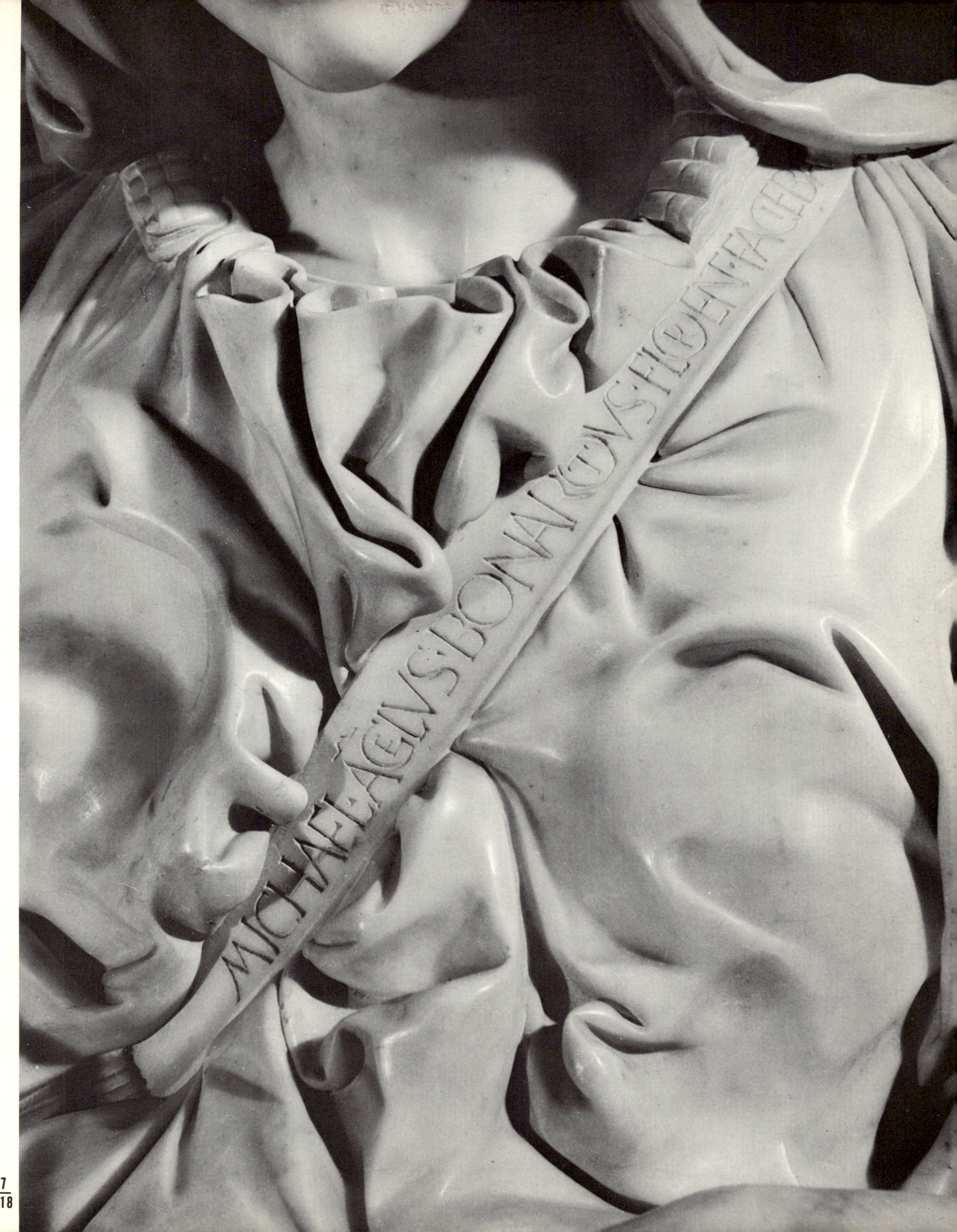

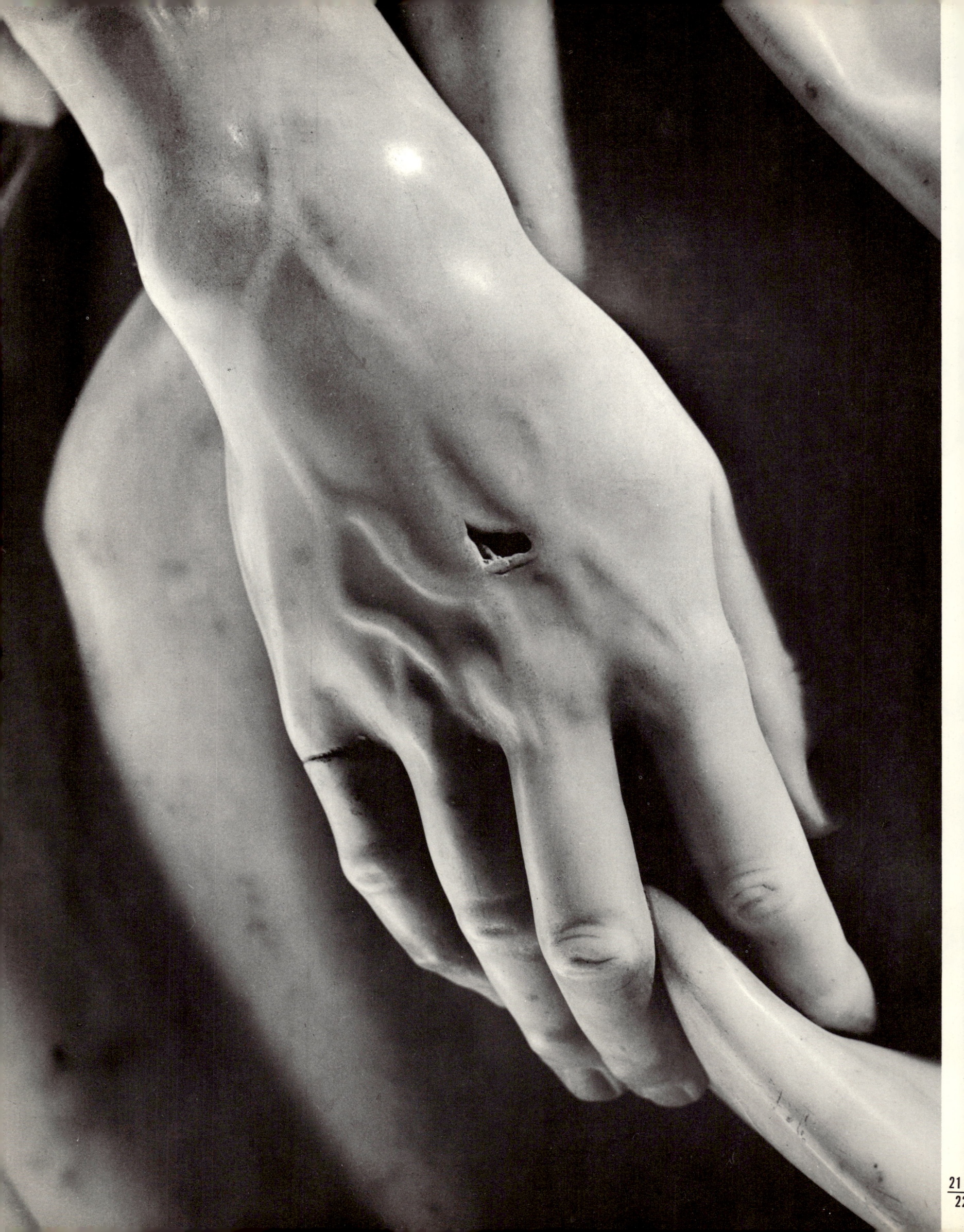

23

24/25

28
29

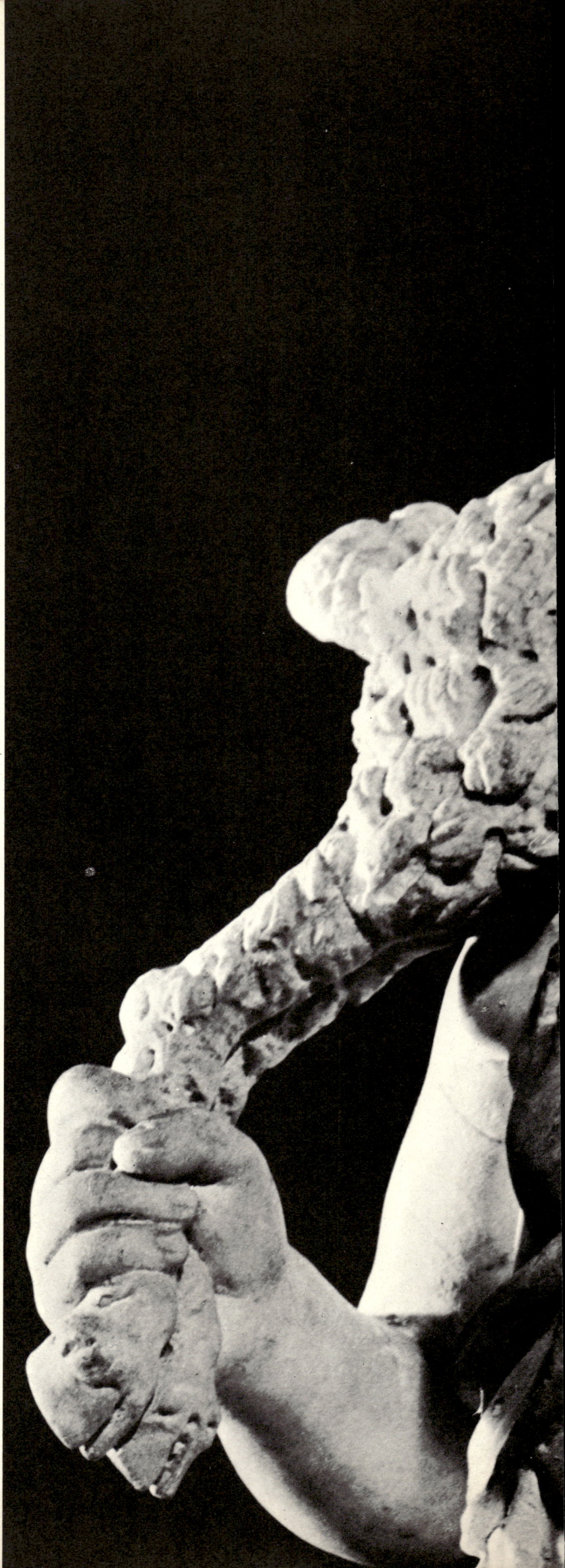

32

33

36

37 ▲

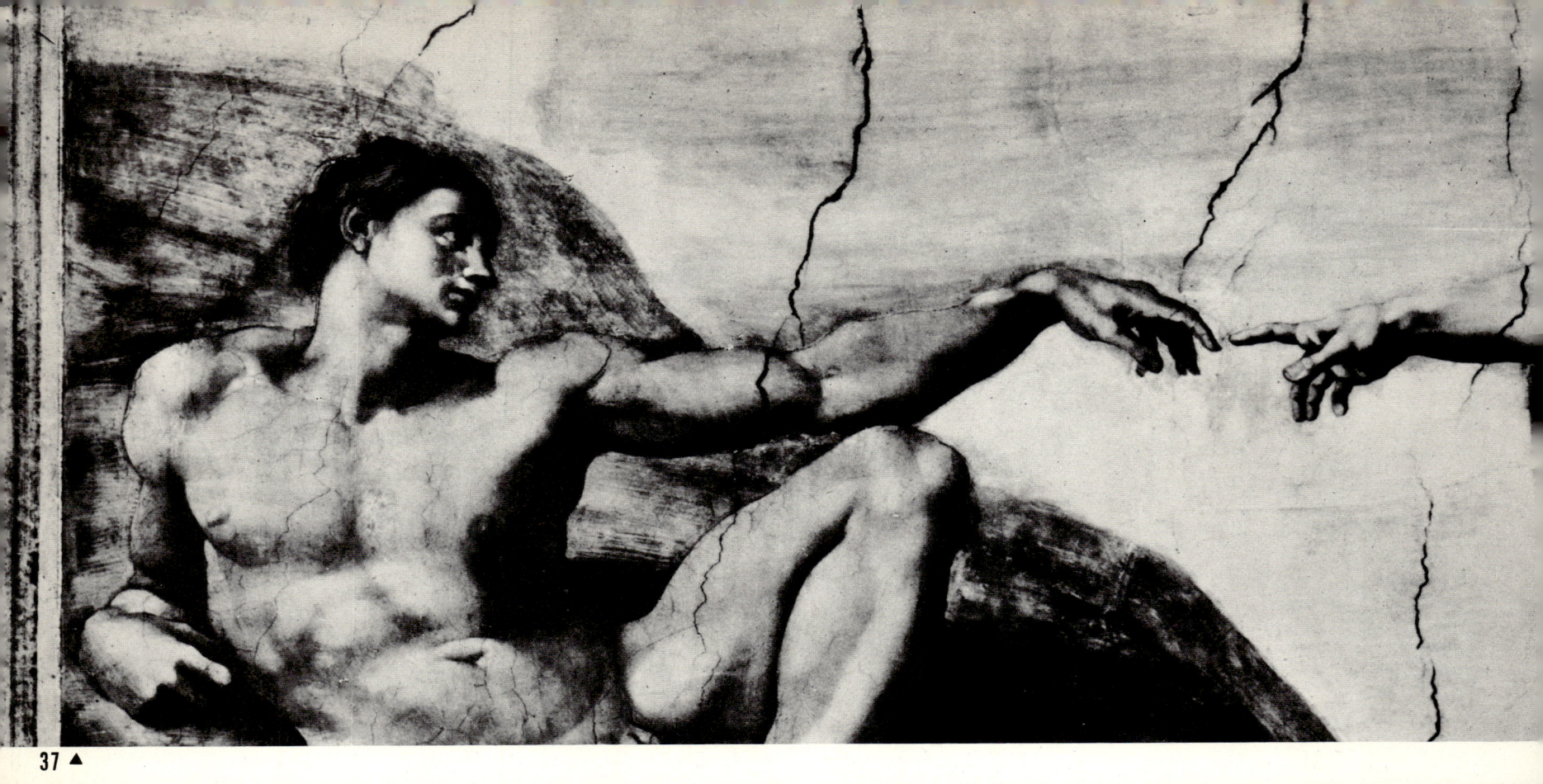

▼ 38

39

▲ 41 ▼

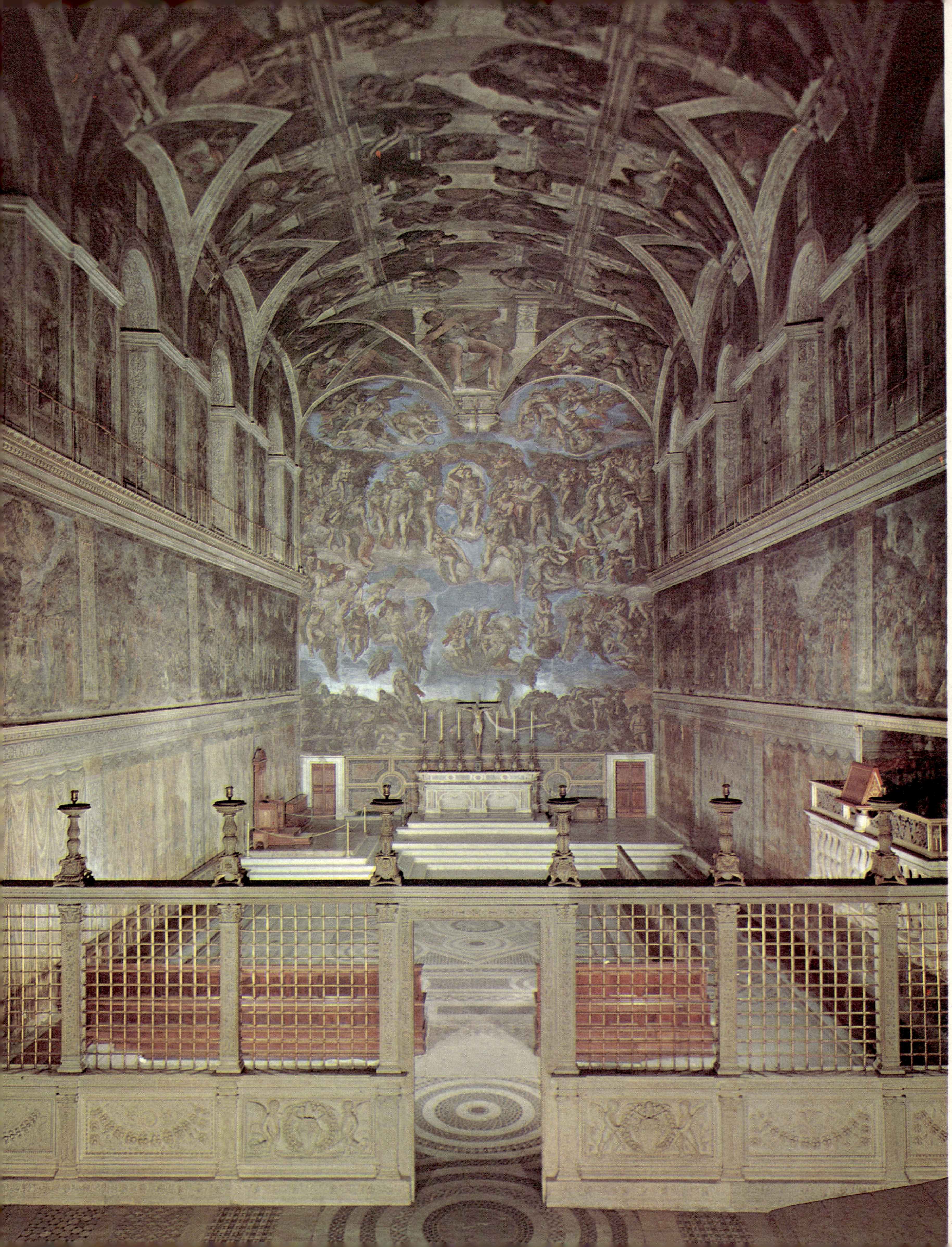

THE SISTINE CHAPEL FOLIO

The Sistine Chapel in the Vatican was designed by Giovanni de Dolci and was constructed between 1475 A.D. and 1483 A.D. during the reign of Pope Sixtus IV. This lovely Chapel is a vital part of the life of the Roman Catholic Church. Not only is it the scene of the most solemn functions held in the presence of the Pope but also of the Conclave of Cardinals when they assemble to choose a new Pope.

Countless artists contributed their skills to the decoration of the Sistine Chapel. Among these were Michelangelo, Ghirlandaio, master of Michelangelo, and Perugina, master of Raphael.

The magnificent paintings of Michelangelo grace the Chapel—the Last Judgment on the wall above the altar, the Fall of the Angels on the wall facing it. The Chapel ceiling or vault, likewise, is a testimonial to the infinite skill and awesome versatility of this artist who began his career as a sculptor and won equal fame with the brush.

The eight-page folio which follows presents details from several of the Chapel's frescoes for the edification and enjoyment of the reader.

44
/
45

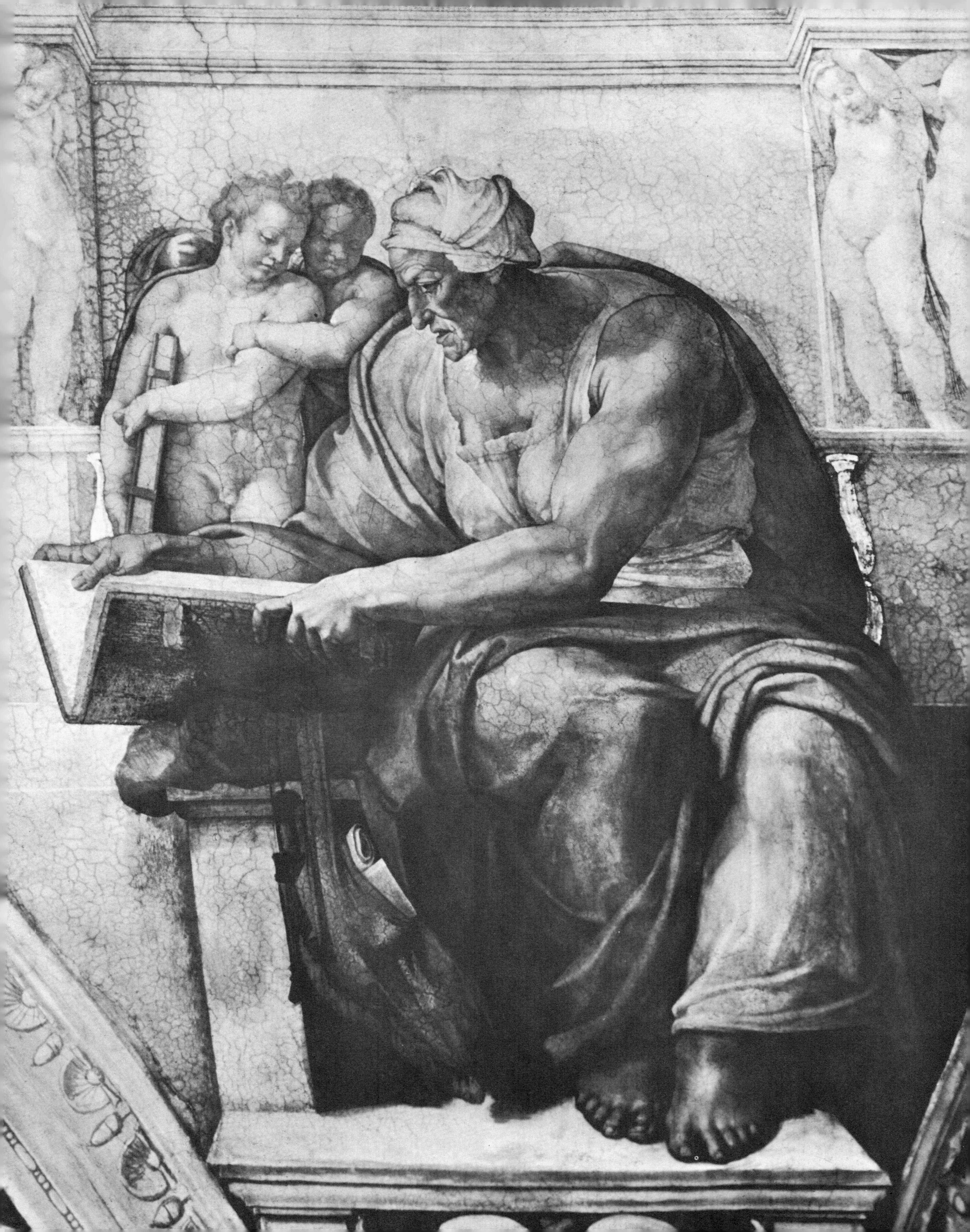

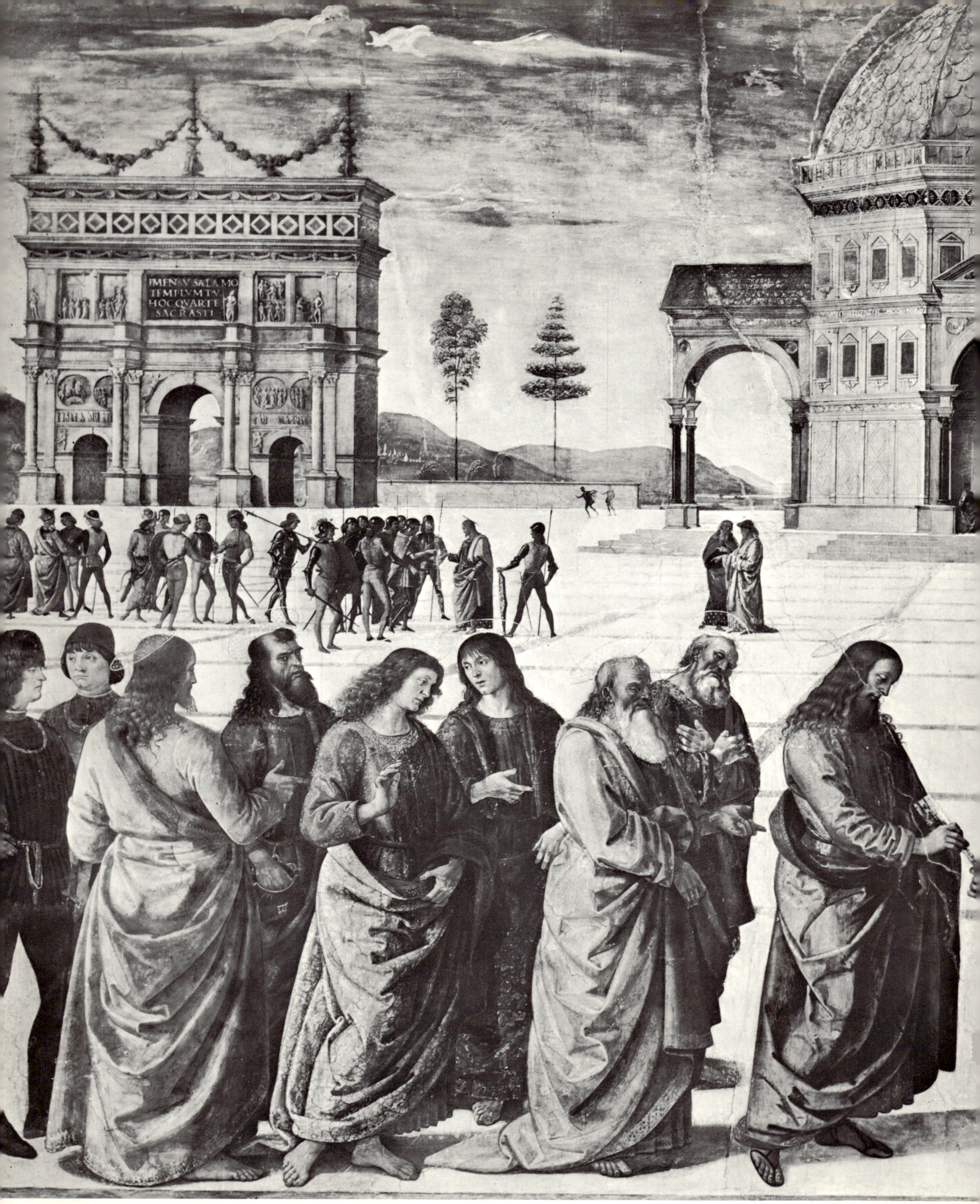
IMENSV SALAMO
TEMPLVM TV
HOC QVARTE
SACRASTI

46

47/48

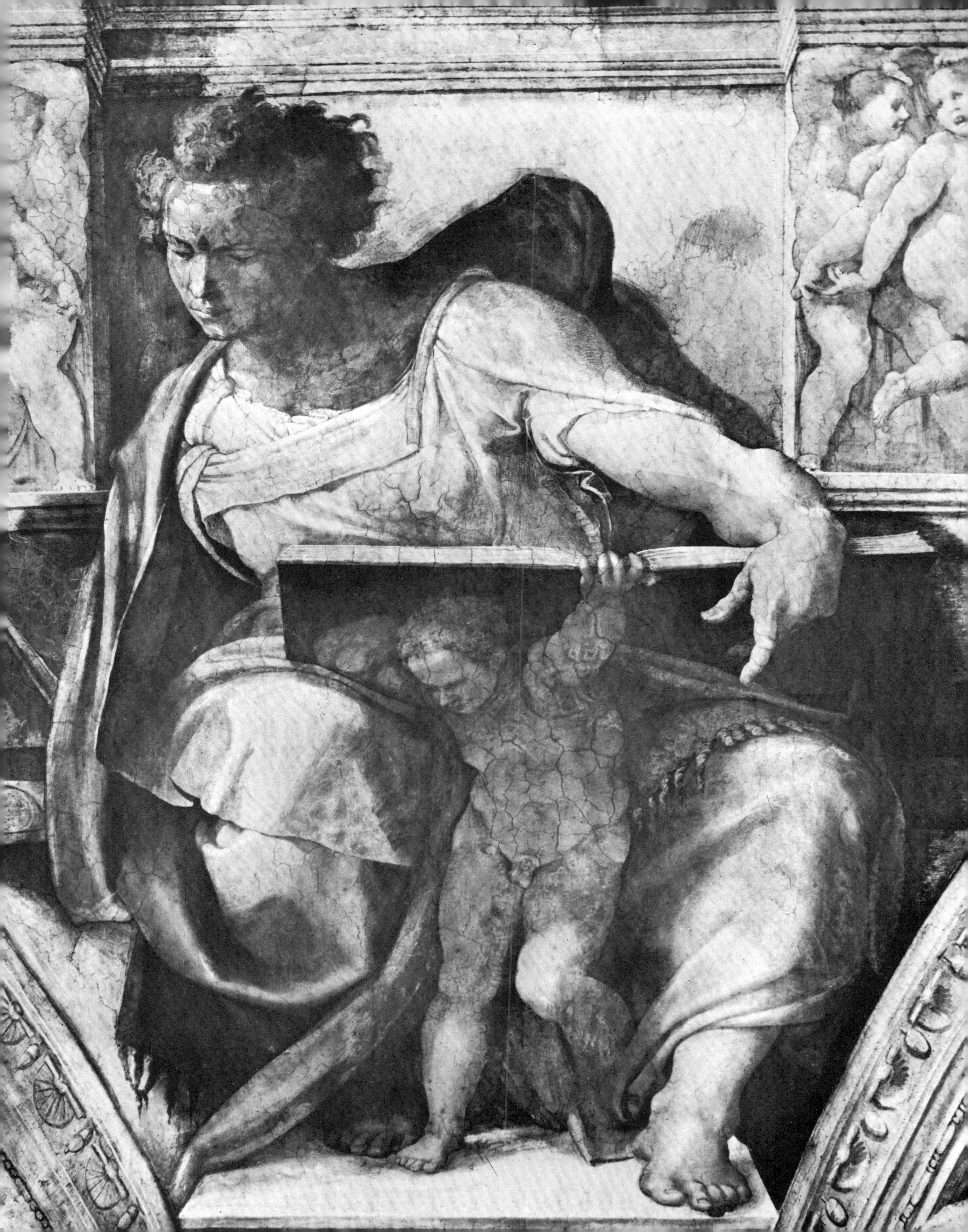

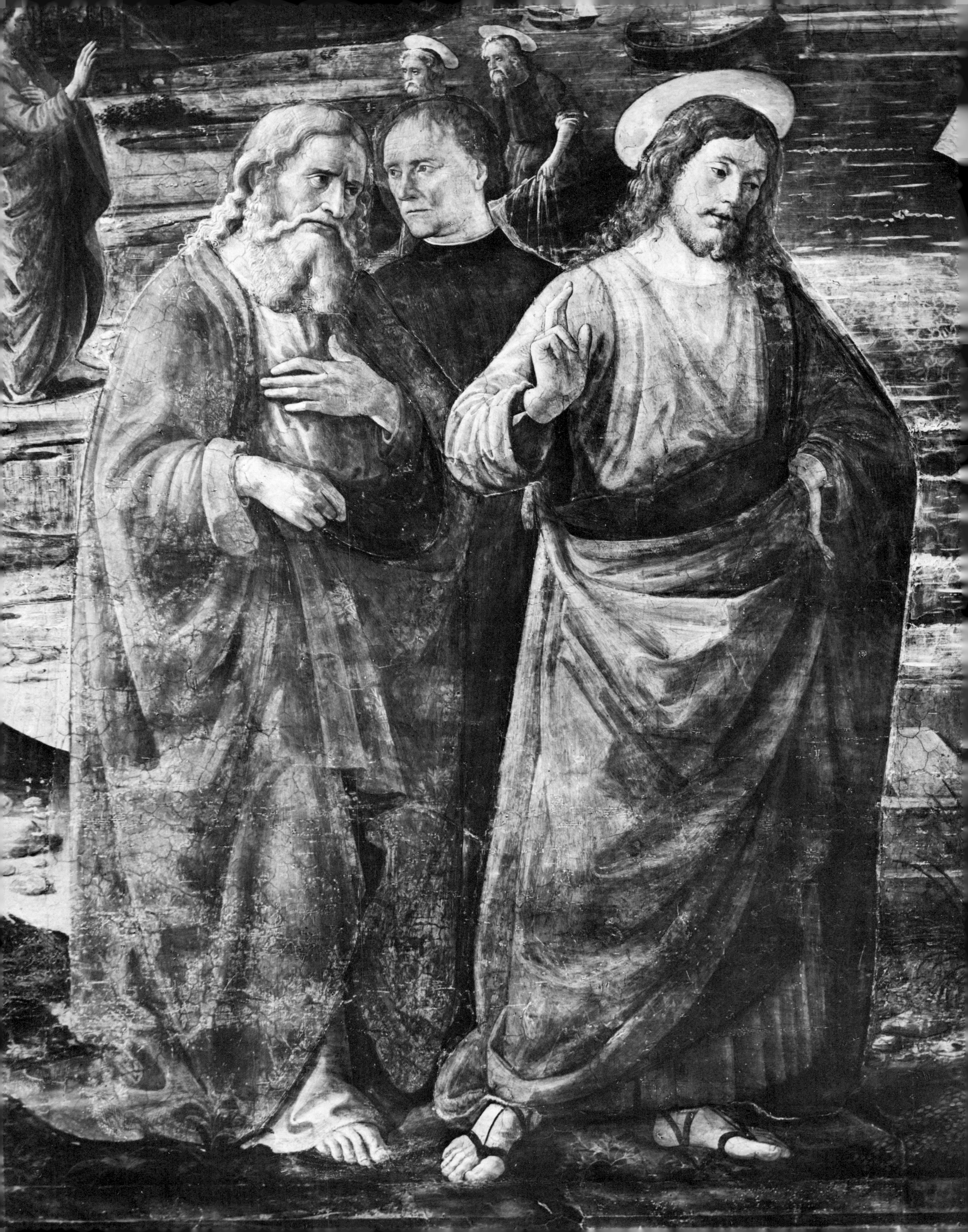

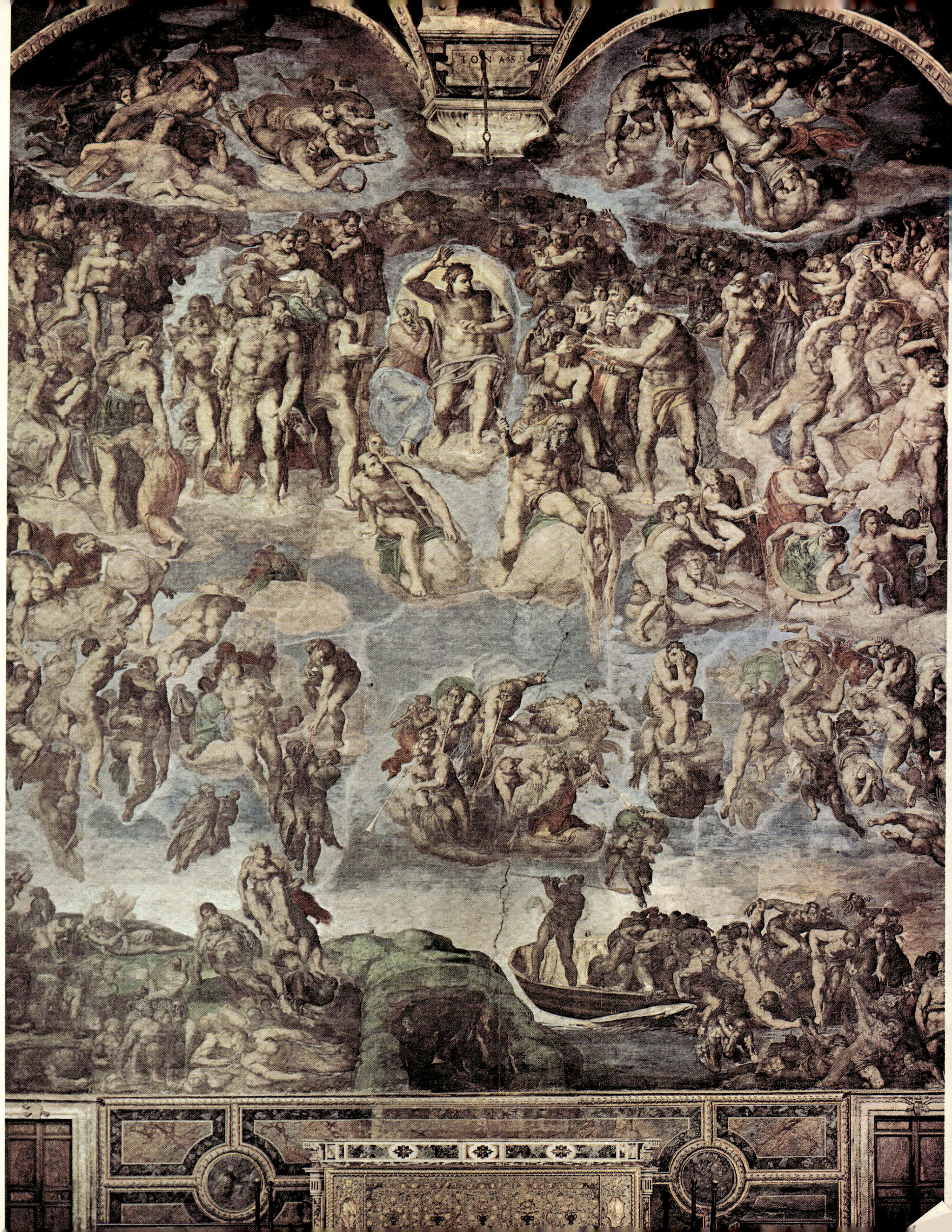
IONAS

51

52

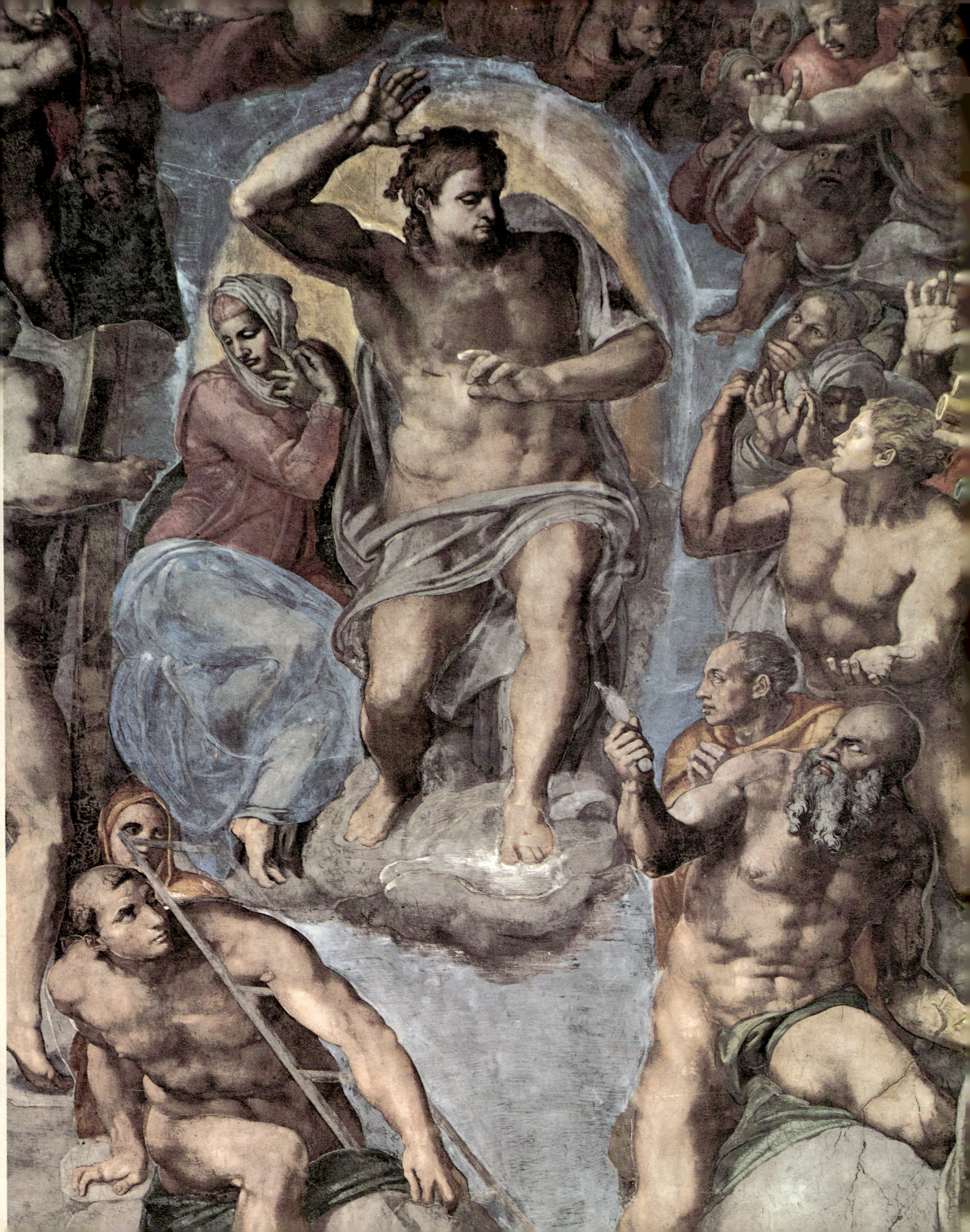

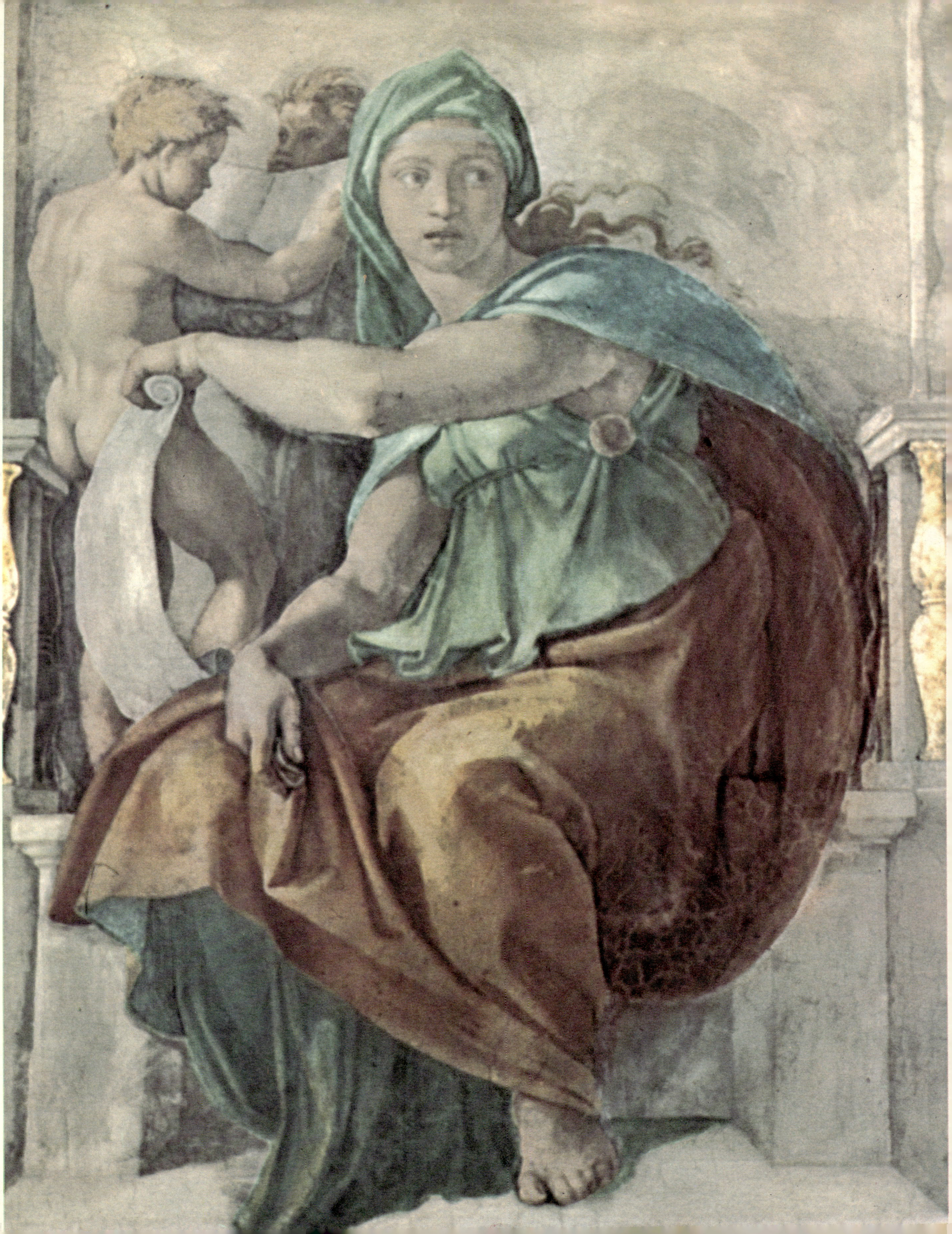

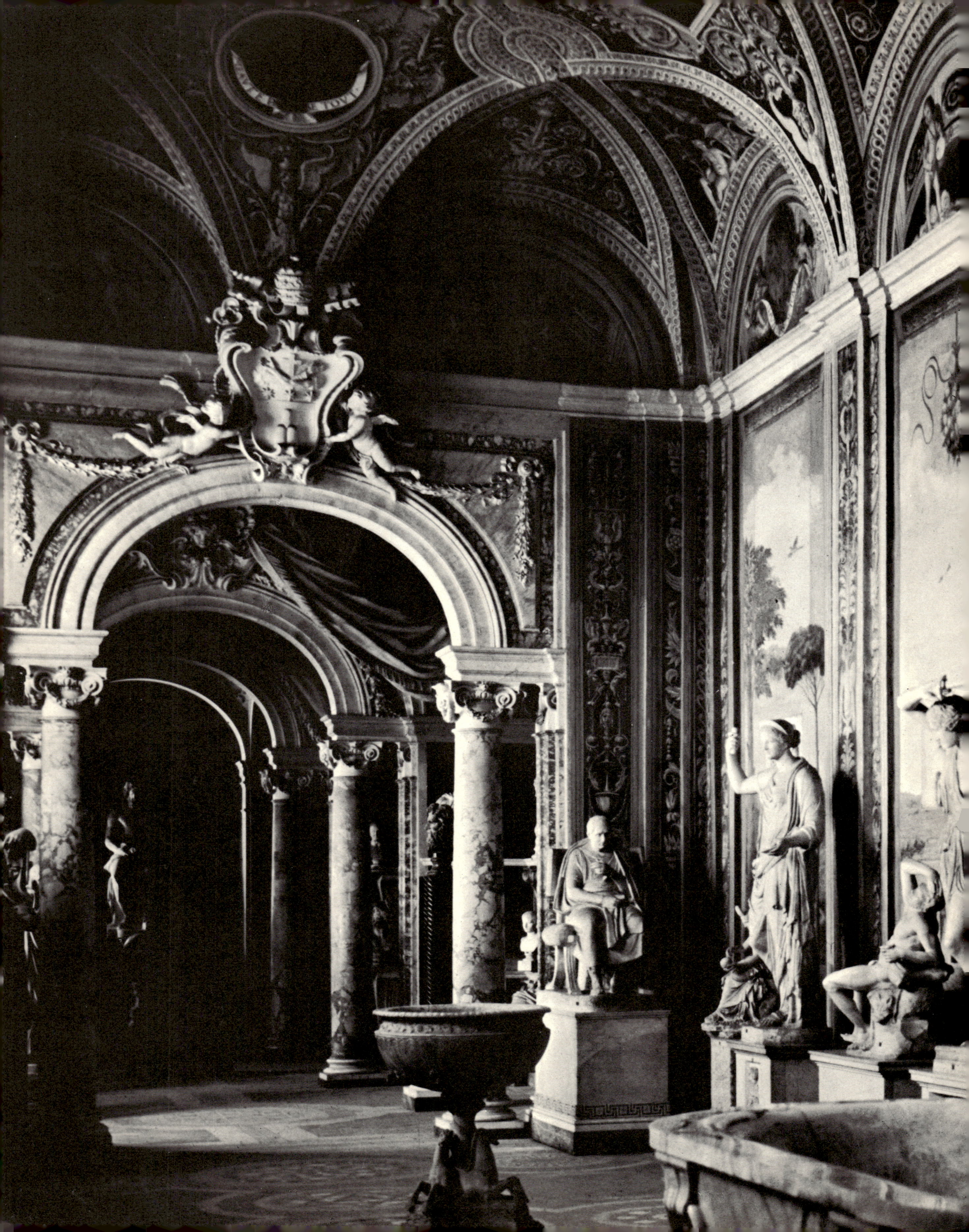

55

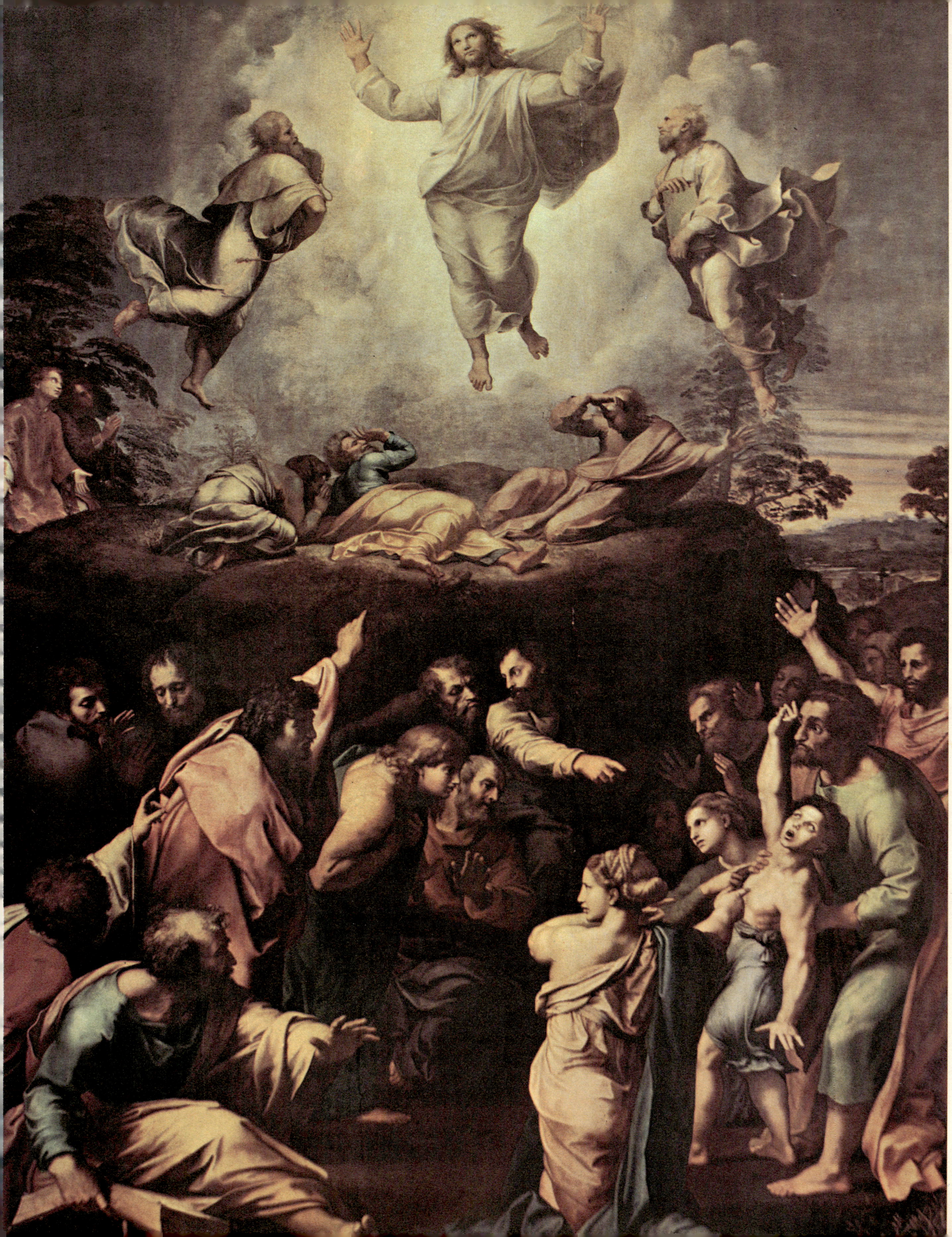

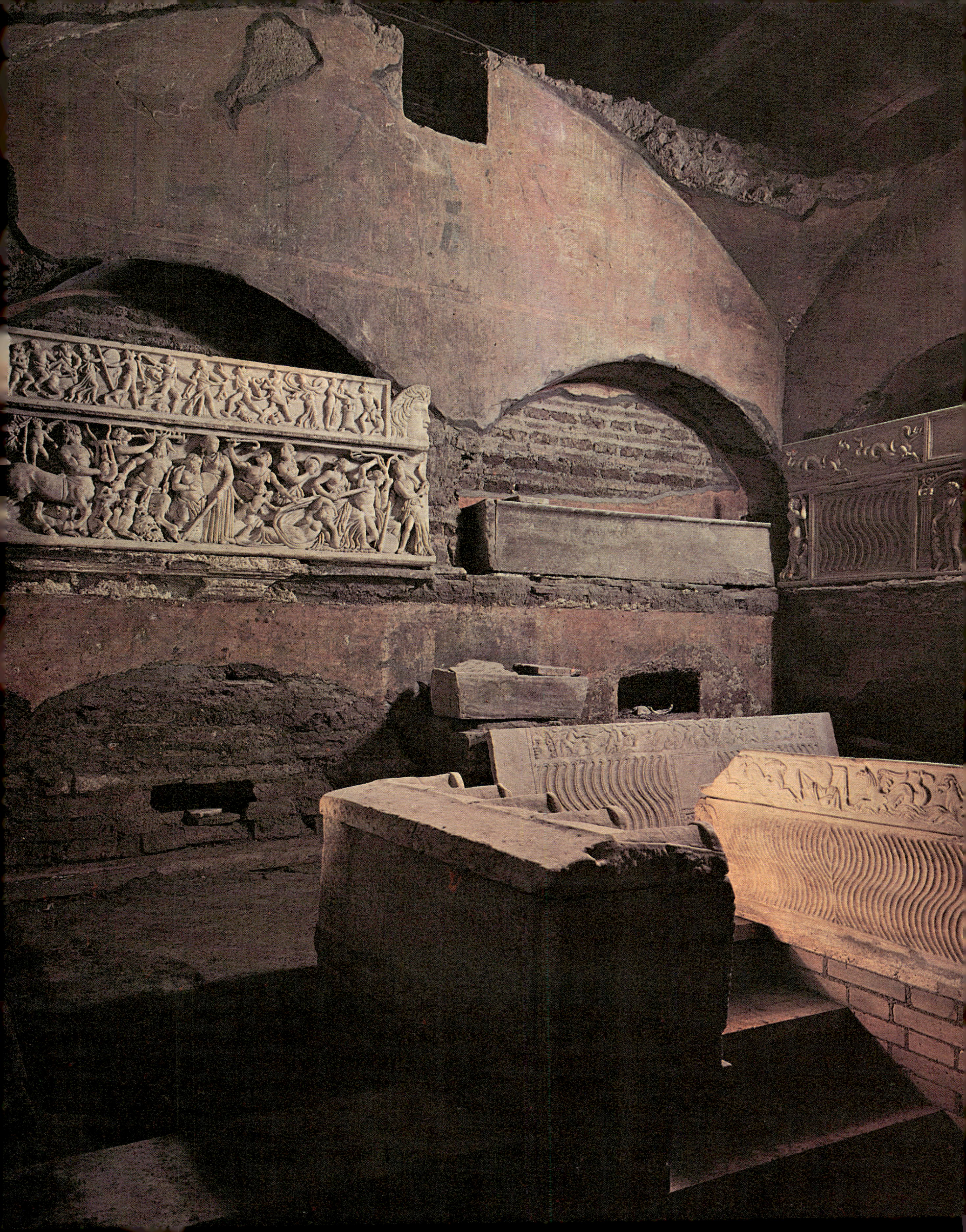

◀ 58

◀ 59

60/61

62/63

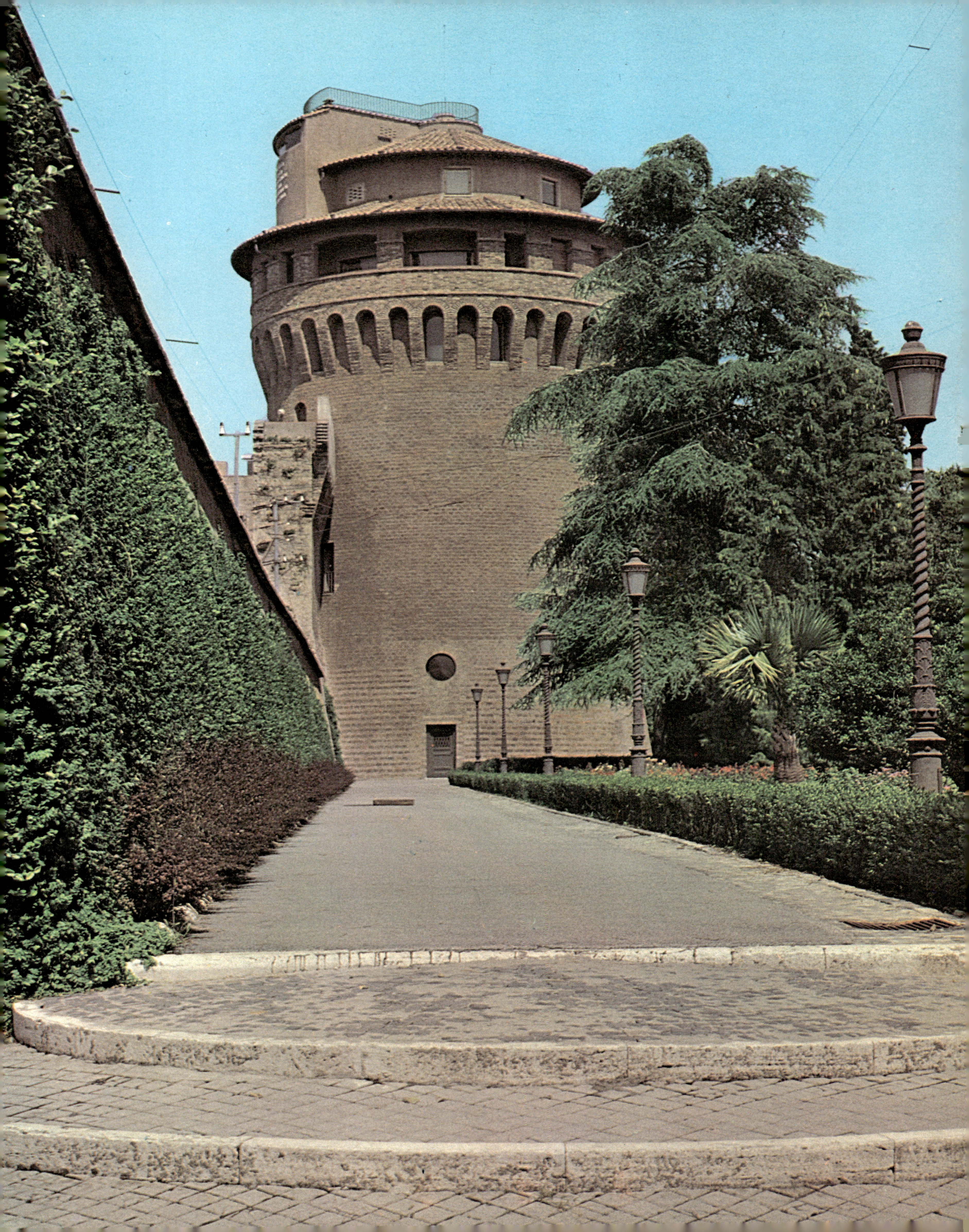

64/65

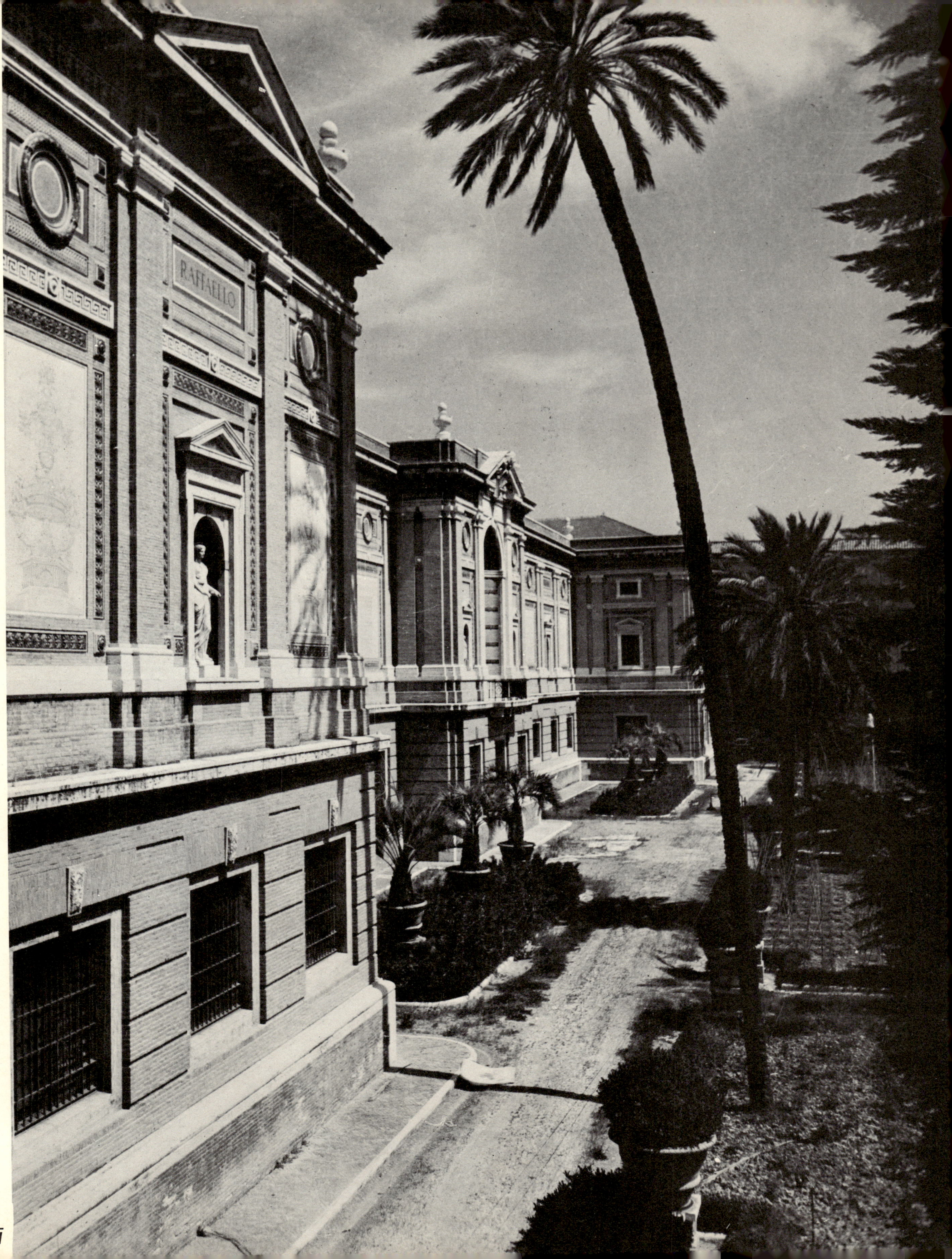
RAFFAELLO

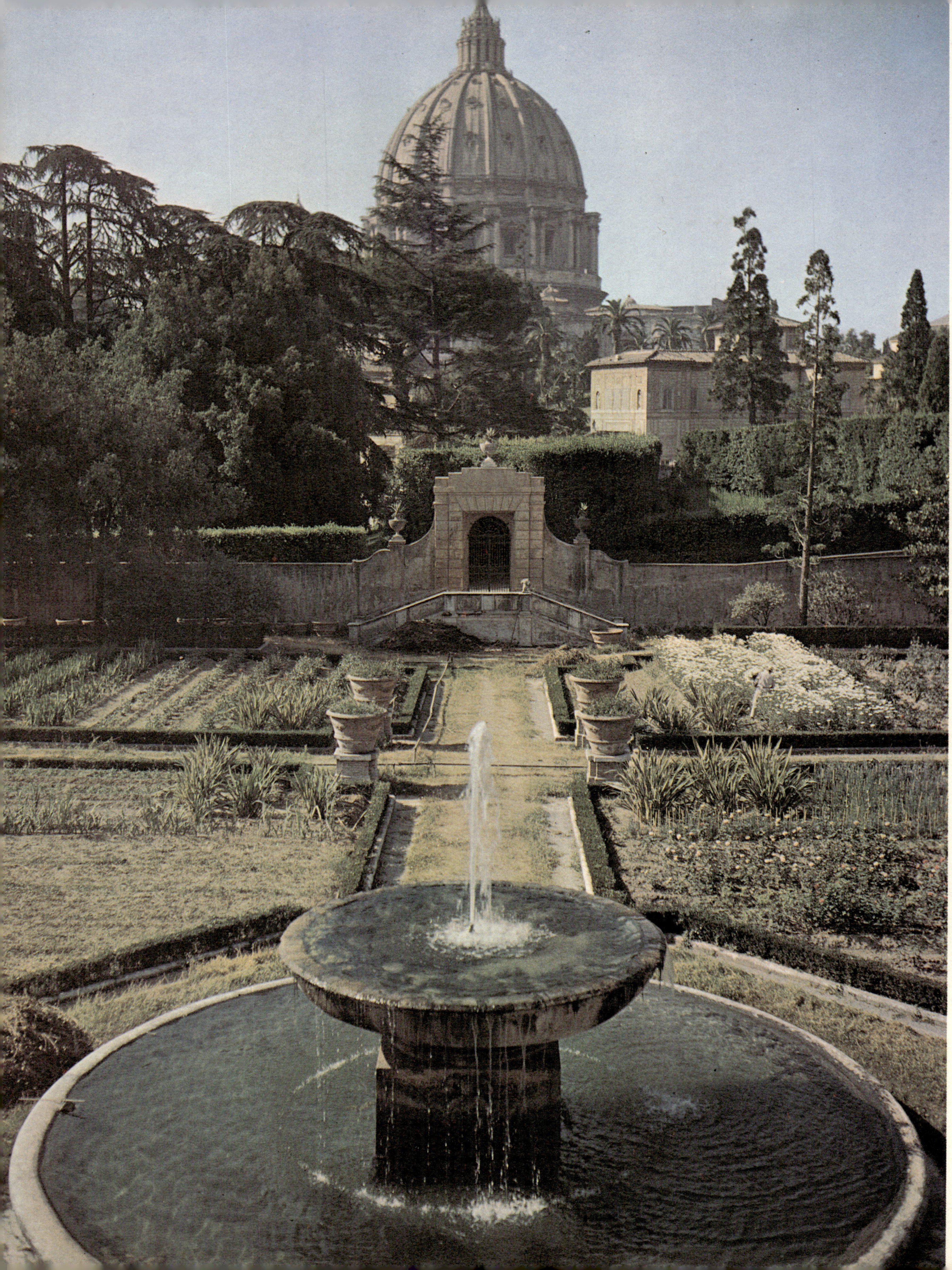

VATIKAN BILDERVERZEICHNIS

BILDERVERZEICHNIS

1. Luftaufnahme von der Vatikanstadt und der Umgebung von Rom. Weit links sieht man das Nordamerikanische Seminar.
2. Der Altar des Papstes—darüber der prachtvolle Baldachin von Bernini.
3. Der hl. Petrus—eine Statue in Bronze (1250-1300 n. Chr.), stammt vermutlich von dem Bildhauer Arnolfo di Cambio.
4. Eine Bronzetür, die mittlere von den fünf grossen Türen, die zum Atrium der St. Peterskirche führen.
5. Der Thron des Papstes (Stuhl des hl. Petrus), das Hauptmerkmal der Altarnische der Basilika, zur Zeit der Seligsprechung von Mutter Seton.
6. Gesamtansicht des Zweiten Vatikanischen Konzils.
7. Papst Paul VI begrüsst John F. Kennedy, den kürzlich verstorbenen Präsidenten der Vereinigten Staaten.
8. Papst Paul VI, im päpstlichen Stuhl, erteilt den Apostolischen Segen am Tage seiner Krönung.
9. Die Schweizer Garde, die Leibgarde der Päpste, beim Ablegen des alljährlichen Eides der Treue zum Heiligen Vater.
10. Seine Heiligkeit, Papst Paul VI, an seinem Schreibtisch im päpstlichen Studierzimmer. Das Bild ist ausschliesslich für dieses Album photographiert worden.
11. Eine Audienz in der Konsistorialhalle im Vatikan Palais. Seine Heiligkeit, Paul VI, auf dem Thron.
12. Der päpstliche Thron in der Halle von Tronetto—einer von den vielen Empfangsräumen im Vatikan Palais.
13. Die Madonna von der Pietà, Michelangelo's Meisterstück.

DAS PIETA FOLIO.

14. *Die Kapelle der Pietà in der Basilika der St. Peterskirche, Rom.*
15. *Die Pietà Gruppe, Ganzaufnahme.*
16. *Die Pietà Gruppe, Teilaufnahme.*
17. *Eine weitere Ansicht von der Madonna von der Pietà.*
18. *Michelangelo's berühmte Inschrift.*
19. *Profile der Madonna und des Christus.*
20. *Das Antlitz Christi.*
21. *Die rechte Hand des Gekreutzigten Christus.*

22. Die fünf amerikanischen Kardinäle auf dem Zweiten Vatikanischen Konzil. Von links nach rechts die Kardinäle: Ritter von St. Louis; McIntyre von Los Angeles; Spellman von New York; Cushing von Boston und Meyer von Chicago.
23. Eine antike Tapete wird in einer Werkstatt das Vatikans ausgebessert.
24. Vatikan's Mosaikatelier, wo die feinsten Mosaikarbeiten hergestellt werden.
25. "Die Bekehrung des hl. Paulus." Eine ergreifende Fresko in der Paulskapelle, gemalt von Michelangelo zwischen 1542 und 1549.
26. "Das Feuer von Borgo," Gemälde von Raphael, hängt in der Kunstgalerie Vatikans.
27. "Der Gute Hirte," zur Zeit ausgestellt in der Kapelle des Vatikanischen Pavillons auf der New Yorker Ausstellung.
28. Diese, aus dem 3. Jh. stammende Statue "Der Gute Hirte", gehört zu den Schätzen des Lateranus Museums in Rom.
29. Der Bildhauer von dem "Guten Hirten" ist unbekannt. Man glaubt jedoch, dass diese Statue die früheste Darstellung Christi ohne Bart ist.
30. Aussicht vom Petersdom. Man sieht den berühmten Säulengang, der den Petersplatz umsäumt. Der Obelisk in der Mitte hat einst den Zirkus Caligula's geschmückt.
31. Ein Ziertisch in einem der vielen Empfangszimmern im Vatikan Palais.
32. Die Kutsche des Papstes Leo XII (18. Jahrhundert).
33. Blick auf eine Ecke des Bernini Baldachins über dem päpstlichen Altar.

34. Die prächtige Scala Regia (Königliche Stiege) führt vom Vatikan Palais in die Basilika.
35. Der Ofen, der für die Verbrennung der für einen neuen Papst abgegebenen Stimmzetteln dient und durch welchen die Ergebnisse der Welt bekannt gegeben werden.
36. Die riesigen Statuen auf der Basilika.
37. "Die Schöpfung des Menschen," eine Teilaufnahme von der Sixtinischen Kapellendecke, von Michelangelo.
38. Die herrliche Decke der Sixtinischen Kapelle—eine Arbeit von Michelangelo.
39. Teilaufnahme von einem Polytychon von Giotto.
40. "Das letzte Abendmahl," abgebildet von einer flämischen Tapete vom 16. Jh. im Vatikan Museum.
41. "Der Heiland und das Märtyrertum des hl. Petrus und hl. Paulus," ein Polytychon von Giotto, zirka 1300 n. Chr.
42. Die wunderschöne Sixtinische Kapelle, deren Name vom Papst Sixtus IV, unter dessen Regierung sie gebaut wurde, abstammt.

DAS FOLIO DER SIXTINISCHEN KAPELLE.

43. *Das Antlitz Jehova's von der "Schöpfung des Menschen," Decke der Sixtinischen Kapelle.*
44. *Prophet Jeremias, Decke der Sixtinischen Kapelle.*
45. *Die Sybille von Cumae, Decke der Sixtinischen Kapelle.*
46. *Jesus gibt die Schlüssel dem hl. Petrus, Fresko von Perugino, Decke der Sixtinischen Kapelle.*
47. *Die stattliche Jugend, Decke der Sixtinischen Kapelle.*
48. *Daniel, der Prophet, Decke der Sixtinischen Kapelle.*
49. *Die Berufung des hl. Petrus und hl. Andreas, von Ghirlandaio, Decke der Sixtinischen Kapelle.*

50. "Das Jüngste Gericht," von Michelangelo, Sixtinische Kapelle.
51. Die Kartenhalle im Vatikan Palais, Ende des 16. Jh. mit Landkarten von verschiedenen Gegenden Italiens ausgestattet.
52. Die Tapetenhalle im Vatikan Palais.
53. Der Donner Gottes, Teilaufnahme vom "Jüngsten Gericht" von Michelangelo.
54. Die Sybille von Delphi, Teilaufnahme von der Decke der Sixtinischen Kapelle.
55. Die Statuenhalle im Vatikan Museum.
56. "Die Verklärung," das letzte Meisterstück von Raphael, in der Kunstgalerie Vatikans.
57. Ruinen von Rom unter der Basilika der Peterskirche.
58. Eine der wichtigsten archäologischen Funde bei der Suche nach dem Grab des hl. Petrus—eine Säule von der Gruft über der Grabstätte.
59. Eine Skizze vom Grab des hl. Petrus.
60. Ehemalige römische Landstrasse, mit Grabstätten an beiden Seiten—ausgegraben unter der Basilika.
61. Der hl. Petrus predigt. Eine Mosaik, die aus dem 8. Jh. stammt und in den Grotten unterhalb der Basilika gefunden wurde.
62. Die Replik des weltberühmten Schreins der hl. Jungfrau von Lourdes, die sich im Vatikan Garten befindet und von Katholiken Frankreichs dem Papst Leo XIII gestiftet wurde.
63. Der Turm des hl. Johannes. Der Turm wurde, auf Wunsch des Papstes Johannes XXIII, zum Teil restauriert und zwar vom Grafen Enrico Galeazzi, Architekt des Heiligen Palais und Generalgoverneur der Vatikanstadt.
64. Die Päpstliche Akademie der Wissenschaft (Halle von Pius IV, 16. Jh.).
65. Springbrunnen der Adler—im Vatikan Garten.
66. Einer von den vielen Springbrunnen in der Vatikanstadt.
67. Verwaltungsgebäude in der Vatikanstadt, errichtet in 1933 während der Regierung des Papstes Pius XI.
68. Blick auf die Kuppeln der Basilika aus den Gärten Vatikans.

★ ★ ★ ★ ★ ★ ★ ★

LE VATICAN

TABLE DES PEINTURES

1. Vue aérienne de la Cité du Vatican et des environs de Rome. Le Collège d'Amérique du Nord se trouve a l'extrême gauche.
2. L'Autel Papal de St. Pierre, surmonté du magnifique baldaquin de Bernini.
3. Statue en bronze de St. Pierre, attribuée au sculpteur Arnolfo di Cambio, et realisée aux environs de 1250 a 1300.
4. La Porte de Bronze au centre des cinq inmenses portes qui s'ouvrent sur l'atrium de St. Pierre.
5. Le Trône Papal (Siège de St. Pierre) qui domine l'abside de la Basilique et dont la photo a eté prise lors de la Béatification de la Mère Seton.
6. Vue d'ensemble d'une session de Deuxième Concile du Vatican.
7. Le Pape Paul VI accueille le dernier President des Etats Unis, John F. Kennedy.
8. Le Pape Paul VI assis sur la Sedia Gestatoria donne, le jour de son couronnement sa Benediction Apostolique.
9. Les Gardes Suisses, garde de corps personnelle des Papes, pretent le serment annuel de fidelité au Saint Père.
10. Sa Sainteté le Pape Paul VI assis au bureau de son cabinet de travail. (La photo a ete prise specialement pour cet album).
11. Une audience dans la Salle Consistoriale du Palais du Vatican. Sa Sainteté Paul VI sur le Trône.
12. Le Trône Papal de la Salle du Tronetto, l'une des nombreuses salles de réception du Palais du Vatican.
13. La Madone de la Pietá, chef d'ouvre de Michel Ange.

LE DEPLIANT DE LA PIETA

14. *La Chapelle de la Pietá (Basilique de St. Pierre à Rome).*
15. *Vue d'ensemble de la Pietá.*
16. *Un détail de la Pietá.*
17. *Un autre aspect de la Madone de la Pietá.*
18. *L'inscription orgueilleuse de Michel Ange.*
19. *Profile de la Madone et du Christ.*
20. *Le visage du Christ de la Pietá.*
21. *La main droite du Christ crucifié de la Pietá.*

22. Les cinq Cardinaux Américains rassemblés au Concile du Vatican. De gauche à droite: Les Cardinaux Ritter, de St. Louis; McIntyre, de Los Angeles; Spellman, de New York; Cushing, de Boston et Meyer, de Chicago.
23. Restauration d'une ancienne tapisserie dans un atelier du Vatican.
24. L'atelier de mosaique du Vatican où l'on fabrique les plus belles mosaiques du monde.
25. La conversion de St. Paul, fresque dramatique de la Chapelle Pauline, peinte par Michel Ange entre 1542 et 1549.
26. L'Incendie de Borgo, d'après Raphaël, Musée du Vatican.
27. Le Bon Pasteur, que l'on peut voir dans la Chapelle du Pavillon du Vatican à l'Exposition Internationale de New York.
28. La Statue du Bon Pasteur qui date du 111e siècle embellit d'ordinaire le Musée Latran à Rome.
29. Le sculpteur du Bon Pasteur est inconnu. On pense que cette statue est la première répresentation du Christ sans barbe.
30. De la coupole de la Basilique on peut admirer la célèbre Colonnade de Bernini que forme la Place St. Pierre. L'Obelisque du centre a orné autrefois, le Cirque de Caligula.
31. Table decorée appartenant a l'une des nombreuses salles d'audience du Palais du Vatican.
32. La Carosse du Pape Leon XIII (18e siècle).
33. Détail d'un coin du baldaquin placé au dessus de l'autel Papal et réalisé par Bernini.

TABLE DES PEINTURES

34. La Scala Regia (Escalièr Royal) qui mène du Palais du Vatican à la Basilique.
35. Le poêle où l'on brûle les bulletins déposés lors de l'élection d'un nouveau Pape; c'est au moyen de ce poêle que les resultats sont révèlés au monde.
36. Les statues gigantesques du sommet de la Basilique.
37. La Creation de l'homme, d'après Michel Ange, détail du Plafond de la Chapelle Sixtine.
38. Le magnifique plafond de la Chapelle Sixtine peint par Michel Ange.
39. Détail d'un polyptyque de Giotto.
40. La Cène, détail d'une tapisserie flamande du XVIe siècle, Musée du Vatican.
41. Le Christ Rédempteur et le martyre de Staints Pierre et Paul, polyptyque de Giotto, fait aux environs de 1300.
42. La Belle Chapelle Sixtine, dont le nom vient de celui du Pontife Sixte IV, sous le règne duquel elle fut batie.

LE DEPLIANT DE LA CHAPELLE SIXTINE

43. *Le visage du Jéhova de la création de l'homme, plafond de la Chapelle Sixtine.*
44. *Le Prophète Jérémie, plafond de la Chapelle Sixtine.*
45. *La Sibylle de Cumes, plafond de la Chapelle Sixtine.*
46. *Jésus remettant le Clés a St. Pierre, fresque de Perugino, à la Chapelle Sixtine.*
47. *Un jeune homme, plein de majesté, plafond de la Chapelle Sixtine.*
48. *Le Prophète Daniel, plafond de la Chapelle Sixtine.*
49. *L'appel de St. Pierre et de St. André d'après Ghirlandaio, détails d'une fresque de la Chapelle Sixtine.*

50. Le Jugement Dernier, d'après Michel Ange, Chapelle Sixtine.
51. La Salle des Cartes, décorée a la fin du XVIe siècle, avec les cartes des diverses region italiennes, Palais du Vatican.
52. La Salle de Tapisseries, Palais du Vatican.
53. La Colère Divine, d'après Michel Ange, détail du Jugement Dernier.
54. La Sibylle de Delphes, détail du plafond de la Chapelle Sixtine.
55. La Salle de Statues; Musée du Vatican.
56. "La Tranfiguration" dernier chef-d'oeuvre de Raphaël, Musée du Vatican.
57. Vestiges Romains découverts dans les grottes sous la Basilique St. Pierre.
58. L'une des découvertes archéologiques les plus importants pendant les recherches du Tombeau de St. Pierre. Une colonne tombale élevée a l'endroit de sa sepulture.
59. Esquisse du Tombeau de St. Pierre, d'après un artiste.
60. Ancienne chaussé romaine avec ses sepultures des deux cotés, découverte sous la Basilique de St. Pierre.
61. St. Pierre prêchant. Mosaïque du VIIIe siècle, découverte dans les grottes qui sont sous la Basilique.
62. La copie du célèbre sanctuaire de Notre Dame de Lourdes, offerte au Pape Léon XIII.
63. La Tour de St. Jean, datant de la première partie de l'ère Chrétienne, restauré en partie par le Comte Enrico Galeazzi, Architecte du Saint Palais et Gouverneur-Général de la Cité du Vatican, a la demand du Pape Jean XXIII.
64. L'Academie Pontificale des Science. (Sale de Pie IV, 6e siècle).
65. La Fontaine des Aigles des Jardins du Vatican.
66. Encore une des nombreuses fontaines de la Cité du Vatican.
67. La Bâtiment Administratif de la Cité du Vatican construit en 1933 sous le règne du Pape Pie XI.
68. Le Dôme de la Basilique vue des Jardins.

★ ★ ★ ★ ★ ★ ★ ★

THE VATICAN PICTORIAL INDEX

PLATE NO.	SUBJECT
1	Aerial view of Vatican City and the surroundings of Rome, with the North American College at far left center.
2	The Papal Altar in St. Peter's, surmounted by the magnificent baldachin by Bernini.
3	Bronze Statue of St. Peter, circa 1250-1300 A.D., attributed to the sculptor Arnolfo di Cambio.
4	The Bronze Door, central of the five huge doors which open into the atrium of St. Peter's.
5	The Papal Throne (Chair of St. Peter), highlight of the apse of the Basilica, at the time of the beatification of Mother Seton.
6	Panorama of the Second Vatican Council in session.
7	Pope Paul VI greets John F. Kennedy, late, lamented President of the United States.
8	Pope Paul VI, seated in the Papal Chair, bestows the Apostolic Blessing on the day of his coronation.
9	The Swiss Guards, personal bodyguards of the Popes, taking their annual oath of allegiance to the Holy Father.
10	His Holiness, Pope Paul VI, at his desk in the papal study in a photograph taken exclusively for this magazine.
11	An audience in the Consistorial Hall in the Vatican Palace, His Holiness, Paul VI, on the throne.
12	The Papal Throne in the Hall of the Tronetto, one of the many reception rooms in the Vatican Palace.
13	The Madonna of the Pieta, Michelangelo's masterpiece.

THE PIETA FOLIO

14	*The Chapel of the Pieta in St. Peter's Basilica, Rome.*
15	*The Pieta group, full view.*
16	*The Pieta group, detail.*
17	*Another view of the Madonna of the Pieta.*
18	*Michelangelo's prideful inscription.*
19	*Profiles of the Madonna and of Christ.*
20	*The face of Christ, from the Pieta.*
21	*The right hand of the Crucified Christ, from the Pieta.*

22	The five American Cardinals assembled for the Vatican Council. Left to right: Cardinals Ritter of St. Louis; McIntyre of Los Angeles; Spellman of New York; Cushing of Boston and Meyer of Chicago.
23	An ancient tapestry is repaired in a Vatican workroom.
24	The Vatican Mosaic studio where some of the finest mosaics in the world are produced.
25	The conversion of St. Paul. Dramatic Pauline Chapel fresco painted by Michelangelo between 1542 and 1549.
26	The Fire of Borgo, painting by Raphael hanging in the Vatican Gallery.
27	The Good Shepherd, on view in the Vatican Pavilion Chapel at the New York World's Fair.
28	Dating from the 3rd Century, the statue of the Good Shepherd normally graces the Lateran Museum in Rome.
29	The sculptor of the Good Shepherd is unknown. The statue is believed to be the earliest representation of Christ without a beard.
30	View from the Dome of St. Peter's, showing the famous colonnade forming St. Peter's Square. The obelisk in the center once adorned Caligula's Circus.
31	Ornate table in one of the multitude of audience rooms in the Vatican Palace.
32	The Coach of Pope Leo XII (18th Century).
33	Detail of a corner of Bernini's baldachin over the Papal Altar.
34	The stately Scala Regia (Royal Stairs) leading into the Basilica from the Vatican Palace.
35	The stove in which the ballots cast for a new Pope are burned — and by which the results are made known to the world.
36	The giant statues atop the Basilica.
37	The Creation of Man, detail from Michelangelo's Sistine Chapel ceiling.
38	The magnificent Sistine Chapel ceiling, the work of Michelangelo.
39	Detail of polyptych by Giotto.
40	The Last Supper, detail from a 16th Century Flemish tapestry in the Vatican Museum.
41	The Holy Redeemer and the martyrdom of Sts. Peter and Paul, a polyptych by Giotto, circa 1300 A.D.
42	The lovely Sistine Chapel whose name is derived from the Pontiff under whose reign it was built, Pope Sixtus IV.

THE SISTINE CHAPEL FOLIO

43	*The Face of Jehovah, from the Creation of Man, Sistine Chapel ceiling.*
44	*The Prophet Jeremiah, Sistine Chapel ceiling.*
45	*The Cumaean Sibyl, Sistine Chapel ceiling.*
46	*Jesus gives the keys to St. Peter, fresco by Perugino, from the Sistine Chapel.*
47	*Stately Youth, Sistine Chapel ceiling.*
48	*Daniel the Prophet, Sistine Chapel ceiling.*
49	*The Calling of Sts. Peter and Andrew by Ghirlandaio, details from a Sistine Chapel fresco.*

50	The Last Judgment by Michelangelo, Sistine Chapel.
51	The Hall of Maps in the Vatican Palace decorated in the late 16th Century with maps of the various regions of Italy.
52	The Hall of Tapestries in the Vatican Palace.
53	The Thunder of God, detail from Michelangelo's Last Judgment.
54	The Delphic Sibyl, detail from the Sistine Chapel ceiling.
55	Hall of the Statues in the Vatican Museum.
56	The last masterpiece of Raphael, "The Transfiguration", from the Vatican Art Gallery.
57	Roman vestiges in the grottoes under the Basilica of St. Peter.
58	One of the most important archeological finds in the search for the grave of St. Peter — a column from the tomb erected over the burial place.
59	An artist's sketch of the Tomb of St. Peter.
60	An ancient Roman roadway with its sepulchres on either side, unearthed under the Basilica.
61	St. Peter preaching. A mosaic from the 8th Century found in the grottoes beneath the Basilica.
62	The replica of the world-famous Shrine of Our Lady of Lourdes in the Vatican gardens, donated to Pope Leo XIII by the Catholics of France.
63	The Tower of St. John, dating from the early Christian era, restored in part by Count Enrico Galeazzi, architect of the Sacred Palace and Governor General of Vatican City, at the request of Pope John XXIII.
64	The Pontifical Academy of Science (Hall of Pius IV, 16th Century).
65	Fountain of the Eagles in the Vatican gardens.
66	Another of the many fountains in Vatican City.
67	Administration Building in Vatican City constructed in 1933 during the reign of Pope Pius XI.
68	View of the Dome of the Basilica from the gardens.

★ ★ ★ ★ ★ ★ ★

EL VATICANO — INDICE PICTORICO

CONTENIDO

1. Vista del aire de la Ciudad del Vaticano y los alrededores de Roma, con el Colegio Norteamericano lejos de la izquierda del centro.
2. Altar Papal en San Pedro, coronado por el baldaquín de Bernini.
3. Estatua en bronce de S. Pedro, circa 1250-1300 A.D., atribuida al escultor Arnolfo di Cambio.
4. Puerta de Bronce, central de las cinco inmensas puertas que se abren en el atrio de S. Pedro.
5. Trono Papa (Silla de S. Pedro), punto de mayor importancia del abside de la Basilica en el tiempo de la beatificación de Madre Seton.
6. Panorama del Segundo Concilio del Vaticano en sesión.
7. Papa Pablo VI saluda a John F. Kennedy, presidente finado de los Estados Unidos.
8. Papa Pablo VI, sentado en la Silla Papal, da la Bendición Apostólica el día de su coronación.
9. Guardias Suizas-guardia personal de los Papas, prestan juramento anual de fidelidad al Santo Padre.
10. Su Santidad Papa Pablo VI, en su escritorio del estudio papal en una fotografia tomada exclusivamente para esta revista.
11. Audiencia en la Sala Consistorial del Palacio del Vaticano, Su Santidad, Pablo VI, en el trono.
12. Trono Papal en la Sala del Tronetto, uno de los numerosos salones de recepción en el Palacio del Vaticano.
13. La Madonna de la Pietà, obra maestra de Miguel Angel.

EL FOLIO DE LA PIETA

14. *Capilla de la Pietà en la Basilica de San Pedro, Roma.*
15. *Vista Completa del grupo de la Pietà.*
16. *Detalle del grupo de la Pietà.*
17. *Otra vista de la Madonna de la Pietà.*
18. *Orgullosa inscripción de Miguel Angel.*
19. *Perfiles de la Madonna y de Cristo.*
20. *Cara de Cristo de la Pietà.*
21. *Mano derecha de Cristo Crucificado de la Pietà.*

22. Los cinco Cardenales Americanos, convocados en el Concilio del Vaticano. De izquierda a derecha: Cardenal: Ritter de St. Louis; McIntyre de Los Angeles; Spellman de Nueva York; Cushing de Boston y Meyer de Chicago.
23. Tapíz antiguo es reparado en un taller del Vaticano.
24. Estudio de Mosaico del Vaticano, donde se producen unos de los mosaicos mas bellos del mundo.
25. La Conversión de San Pablo, dramático fresco de la Capilla Paulina, pintado por Miguel Angel entre 1542 y 1549.
26. El Fuego de Borgo, pintura de Rafael, expuesta en la Galeria del Vaticano.
27. El Buen Pastor, expuesto en la capilla del Pabellón del Vaticano, en la Feria Mundial de Nueva York.
28. Estatua del Buen Pastor, que data del siglo tercero, que generalmente adorna el Museo Lateranense en Roma.
29. El escultor del Buen Pastor es desconocido, se cree que la estatua es la primera representación de Cristo sin barba.
30. Vista de la Cúpula de San Pedro, que muestra la famosa columnata que forma la Plaza de San Pedro. El obelisco al centro que adornó una vez el Circo de Caligula.
31. Mesa Ornada en uno de los numerosos salones de audiencia en el Palacio del Vaticano.
32. Coche del Papa Leon XII, siglo XVIII.
33. Detalle de una esquina del baldaquín sobre el Altar Papal.
34. La majestuosa Scala Regia (Escalera Real), que conduce a la Basilica del Palacio del Vaticano.
35. Estufa en la cual se queman los votos dados para la elección de un nuevo Papa-y por medio de la cual se revela el resultado al mundo.
36. Gigantescas estatuas, en la parte superior de la Basilica.
37. La Creación del Hombre, detalle tomado del techo de la Capilla Sixtina de Miguel Angel.
38. El techo de la magnifica Capilla Sixtina, obra de Miguel Angel.
39. Detalle de una poliptica de Giotto.
40. La Ultima Cena, detalle tomado de un tapiz flamenco del siglo XVI, del museo del Vaticano.
41. El Santo Redentor y el matírio de San Pedro Y San Pablo, poliptica de Giotto, circa 1300 A.D.
42. La bella Capilla Sixtina, cuyo nombre deriva del Pontifice Papa Sixto IV, en cuyo reinado fué construida.

FOLIO DE LA CAPILLA SIXTINA

43. *Cara de Jehova, de la Creación del Hombre, techo de la Capilla Sixtina.*
44. *El Profeta Jeremias, techo de la Capilla Sixtina.*
45. *La Sibila de Cumas, techo de la Capilla Sixtina.*
46. *Jesus da las llaves a San Pedro, fresco de Perugino, de la Capilla Sixtina.*
47. *Joven majestuoso, techo de la Capilla Sixtina.*
48. *Daniel el Profeta, techo de la Capilla Sixtina.*
49. *La Llamada de San Pedro y San Andrés de Ghirlandaio, de la Capilla Sixtina.*

50. El Juicio Final de Miguel Angel, Capilla Sixtina.
51. Sala de Mapas en el Palacio del Vaticano, decorada en el siglo XVI, con mapas de las diversas regiones de Italia.
52. Sala de Tapices en el Palacio del Vaticano.
53. El Trueno del Juicio Final, detalle del Juicio Final de Miguel Angel.
54. La Sibila Délfica, detalle del techo de la Capilla Sixtina.
55. Sala de Estatuas en el Museo del Vaticano.
56. La ultima obra maestra de Rafael, "La Transfiguración", de la Galeria de Arte del Vaticano.
57. Vestigios Romanos en las grutas debajo de la Basilica de San Pedro.
58. Uno de los descubrimientos arqueológicos mas importantes en la búsqueda de la tumba de San Pedro-una columna de la tumba erigida sobre la sepultura.
59. Diseno de un artista de la Tumba de San Pedro.
60. Antigua carretera Romana con sepulturas en ambos lados, descubierta abajo de la Basilica.
61. San Pedro predica, Mosaico del siglo VIII, hallado en las grutas abajo de la Basilica.
62. Duplicado de la mundialmente famosa Gruta de Nuestra Señora de Lourdes en los jardines del Vaticano, donado al Papa Leon XIII por los Católicos de Francia.
63. La Torre de San Juan, que data de la primera era Cristiana, restituida en parte por el Conde Enrico Galeazzi, arquitecto del Santo Palacio y Gobernador General de la Ciudad del Vaticano, a solicitud del Papa Juan XXIII.
64. Academia Pontifical de Ciencia (Sala de Pio IV, Siglo XVI).
65. Fuente de las Aguilas en los jardines del Vaticano.
66. Otra de las numerosas fuentes en la ciudad del Vaticano.
67. Edificio de Administración de la Ciudad del Vaticano, construido en 1933, durante el reinado del Papa Pio XI.
68. Vista de la Cupula de la Basilica desde los jardines.

★ ★ ★ ★ ★ ★ ★

INSIDE: PICTORIAL INDEX IN ENGLISH and FRENCH; GERMAN and ITALIAN INDICES FOLLOW